AF439564

THE ENDANGERED MAMMALS

FROM AROUND THE WORLD

ANIMAL BOOKS FOR KIDS AGE 9-12

Children's Animal Books

Many mammal species are in danger! How did this happen, and what can we do about it? Let's find out!

Wild elephant.

HOW DO SPECIES BECOME ENDANGERED?

There are more than thirty million animal species on our Earth. We know there were other species in the past that have become extinct for various reasons. Perhaps their food source ran out, or they were hunted until there were no more left.

This was a regular and expected event in the story of our planet. But in recent times, as humans have become the most dominant species, more and more of the other species are becoming extinct faster and faster. Humans use up the land, trap, shoot, or poison animals, and destroy animal habitats to build roads or mine for minerals.

Eyes of a tiger.

The human "footprint" on the Earth is heavy, and no one person thinks that he or she is the one causing damage to the Earth. But we all need to tread more lightly and pay more attention to how the way we live affects how other creatures live—if they are even able to continue living at all!

As habitats shrink, the climate changes, and their food sources get smaller, mammals who can't adapt, start to die out. As they get closer to dying out, we call a species *"endangered"*. Learn more about animals at risk in the Baby Professor book *Vulnerable, Endangered, and Critically Endangered Animals: What are They?*

Addax (Addax nasomaculatus)

THE MOST ENDANGERED MAMMALS

Here are some of the world's most endangered mammals.

ADDAX

The Addax, or white antelope, lives in Africa's Sahara Desert. Its coat changes color according to the season, to help it hide from predators. But it is a slow runner, and easy prey for animals and human trophy hunters. There are fewer than two thousand addax left.

MONK SEAL

There are two monk seal species that we still have, as many other seals of this type are already extinct. One species lives in the Mediterranean; the other in the waters around Hawaii. They are losing habitat, are often poisoned by pollution from factories and farms, and are caught in fishing nets. People also hunt them for their skins. There are now fewer than two thousand monk seals.

Mediterranean Monk Seal.

MOUNTAIN GORILLA

Y ou have probably seen pictures of this African gorilla. It has longer fur than other gorillas, so it can live in both warm and colder climates. They have been hunted for meat, as trophies, and because people fear they might attack children in new villages. There are fewer than one thousand still in the wild.

Mountain Gorilla (Gorilla beringei beringei) in the jungle, Rwanda.

ISLAND FOX

The island fox lives in packs on the six Channel Islands off the coast of California. Only about seven hundred of this colorful fox are still in the wild.

Santa Cruz Island Fox (Urocyon littoralis santacruzae).

BACTRIAN CAMEL

Bactrian camels are the ones with two humps. Their home area includes Mongolia and China, but they travel widely so there are groups in India, Russia, and Pakistan. But each group is very small now, and there are fewer than one thousand in all.

Bactrian Camel in the steppes of Mongolia.

AMUR LEOPARD

The Amur leopards live in Russia near the border with China. People hunt them for their skins, and that and reduction of their habitat has reduced their numbers in the wild to under 400.

Amur Leopard.

SUMATRAN RHINOCEROS

The Indonesian island of Sumatra is rich in wildlife and, unfortunately, has a lot of endangered species. Harvesting of the forests and expansion of towns is dramatically reducing habitat. This, the smallest of rhinoceros species, is down to under 300 individuals not in zoos or preserves.

Sumatran Rhinoceros (Dicerorhinus Sumatrensis).

IBERIAN LYNX

The lynx, which lives in Spain and Portugal, is very close to extinction. If it dies out, it will be the first feline species to become extinct in modern history.

JAVA RHINOCEROS

Java, in Indonesia, is home to this rhino, which is hunted for its horns and some internal organs. They are used to make traditional Chinese medicine. Fewer than 100 of these rhinos still live in the wild.

Iberian Lynx (Lynx pardinus) lying down.

BROWN SPIDER MONKEY

This long-tailed acrobat lives in Colombia and Venezuela, and is hunted for meat, to sell as a pet or zoo specimen, and to keep it away from farms and gardens. There are only about fifty left.

Brown Spider Monkey.

MEXICAN WOLF

There are fewer than 400 of these wolves left, and almost all of them are now in captivity. The decline in the population of deer and elk in their part of Mexico led to a dramatic drop in their population.

BAIJI DOLPHIN

Baiji dolphins used to be plentiful in the Yangtze River in China, but a combination of hunting and pollution has almost wiped them out. There may be fewer than 20 left outside of aquariums and research facilities.

Mexican Gray Wolf (Canis lupus).

NORTHERN WHITE RHINOCEROS

There are fewer than ten of these rhinos left, and none of them are in their traditional African habitat. They live in wildlife centers, under round-the-clock armed guard. Poachers can make big money by selling rhino horns for use in traditional medicines.

White Rhino.

Assateague Sika Deer.

HELP PRESERVE ENDANGERED SPECIES

Many governments have started programs to try to protect endangered species, and even help their numbers grow again in the wild. Some of these programs have been very successful and some animals have been removed from the *"endangered"* list. However, researchers believe that many more species are in danger than those officially entered on the list.

The process of getting a species recognized as *"endangered"* takes over two years, and often there are interests opposed to the listing. People who want to hunt a particular kind of animal, whether for its meat or as a trophy, don't like the idea of the government trying to protect it.

Here are some things you can do to learn more about, and help to preserve, endangered mammal species near where you live:

- **LEARN.** Find out about endangered species near you, and what is threatening them. Websites like endangered.fws.gov can provide interesting information.

- **SHARE.** Tell family members and friends about these animals, what they contribute to the environment, and what is threatening their existence.

Lioness tagged with tracking device.

- **VISIT A WILDLIFE HERITAGE**, animal refuge, or other protected area. Learn what the staff can tell you about animals in danger and what the facility is trying to do to protect them and help them flourish. To find a wildlife refuge in the United States, check the website fws.gov/refuges/.

Bull Moose eating willows at the Arapaho National Wildlife Refuge, Colorado

- **SECURE.** Is your home wildlife-friendly? Make sure your garbage is not somewhere where animals might eat, and be poisoned by, what you are throwing out. Feed your pets indoors. Cut down on water use so more fresh water is available in the wild. Keep birds from banging into picture windows by putting decals on the windows—millions of birds die this way every year.

- **PLANT.** Plant bushes, trees, and plants around your home that are native to your area. Your local birds, insects, and animals rely on then! Exotic plants may drive out the native ones, so don't put them in your garden even if they are very pretty.

- **AVOID SPRAYS.** Pesticides can kill all the insects that plants need for pollination and that birds need to eat. Herbicides can kill not just the weeds you want to get rid of but other plants that are essential to your local ecosystem. This website shares some alternatives to pesticides: www.beyondpesticides.org.

Persian Fallow Deer (Dama dama mesopotamica)..

- **SLOW DOWN.** Lots of endangered animals die because cars run into them. Especially in the early morning and late afternoon, drive more slowly so you can avoid wildlife that needs to cross your path.

- **BUY SUSTAINABLY.** Humans use the natural environment much faster than it can restore itself. Animals rely on what we are using up, cutting down, or burning. If you buy products made of recycled materials, grown locally, and packaged without a lot of wasteful plastic, you can reduce pressure on the environment. Avoid products made from rare woods from harvesting rainforests, and palm oil produced in plantations where there used to be animal habitats.

- **AVOID SUPPORTING THE HUNTERS.** Don't buy souvenirs made from endangered species, including anything made from ivory, tortoise shell, or coral.

Pelts of fur animals hang on a rope

- **BE GENTLE.** It is illegal and cruel to harass wildlife, and it is a crime to harm an animal of a species identified as endangered. Leave them alone and let them get on with their lives as best they can.

Matching Isolated Ivory Tusks.

- **ADD YOUR VOICE.** You are just one person. But if you tell other people that saving the environment is important to you, they may start to think more seriously about it.

- **JOIN IN!** There are groups near you working to preserve the environment, help animals flourish, reduce pollution, and make a better life for both humans and animals. Find out what is happening nearby and see if what one of the groups is doing is something you would like to help with. They would be very happy to have you join the effort!

A rhino missing its horn in Chitwan National park. A protected animal.

OUR PRECIOUS WORLD

We are part of the family of life on the Earth. Of all the creatures, we are in the best position to protect species and our environment. Learn more about the challenges we face in Baby Professor books like *What Every Child Should Know About Climate Change.*

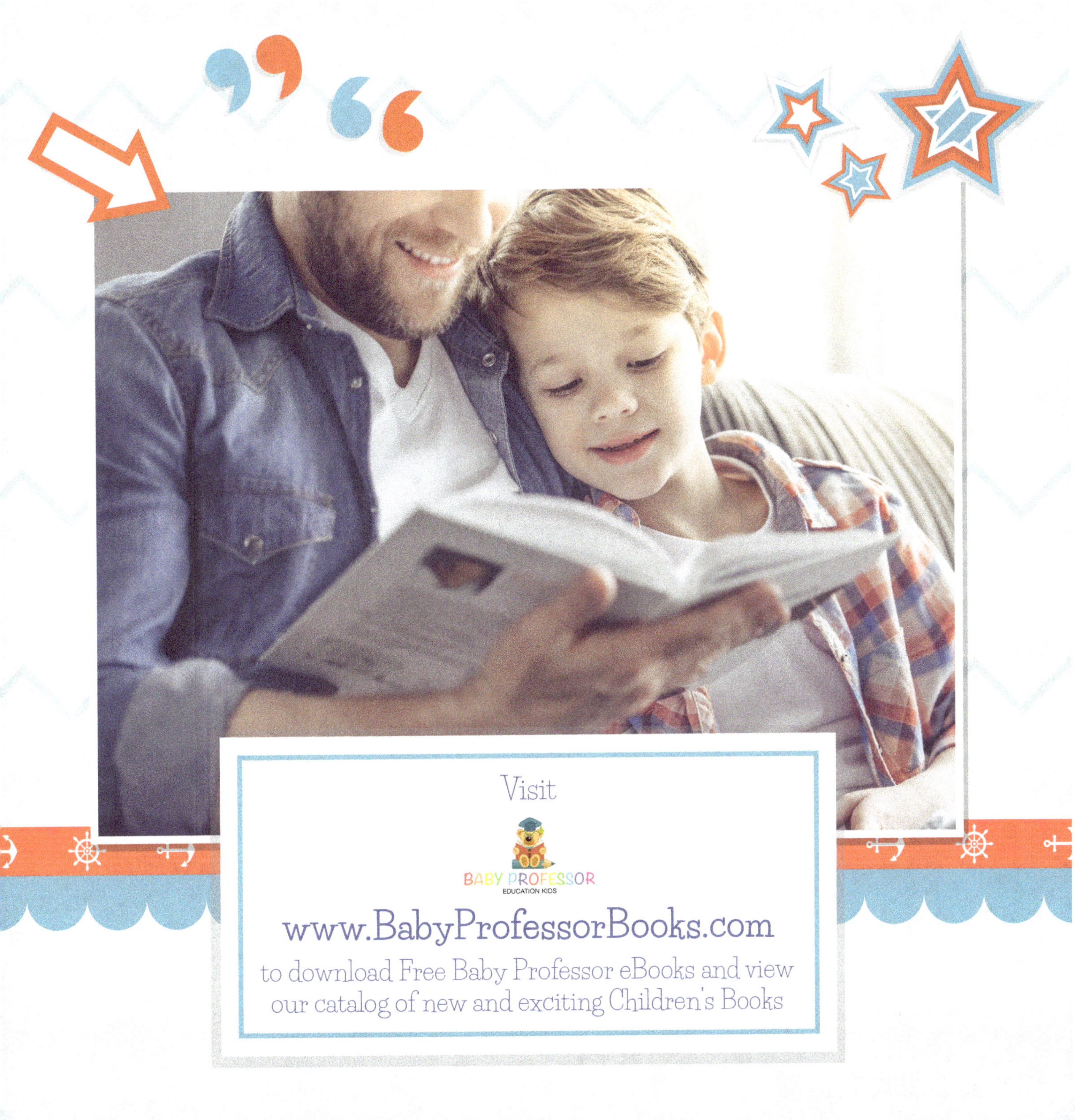

Visit

BABY PROFESSOR
EDUCATION KIDS

www.BabyProfessorBooks.com

to download Free Baby Professor eBooks and view
our catalog of new and exciting Children's Books